D0948941

My Favorite Machines

Helicopters

Colleen Ruck

A⁺

Smart Apple Media

Smart Apple Media
P.O. Box 3263, Mankato, MN 56002

 An Appleseed Editions book

Planning and production by Discovery Books Limited
Designed by D.R ink
Edited by Colleen Ruck

Library of Congress Cataloging-in-Publication Data

Ruck, Colleen.
 Helicopters / by Colleen Ruck.
    p. cm. -- (My favorite machines)
 Includes index.
 ISBN 978-1-59920-675-2 (library binding)
 1. Helicopters--Juvenile literature. I. Title.
 TL716.2.R83 2012
 629.133'352--dc22
                              2011010308

Photograph acknowledgments
European Air Crane: pp. 12, 13; Getty Images: p. 17 (Luis Acosta/AFP); Istockphoto.com: p. 21; Shutterstock: pp. 4 (Maxim Petrichuk), 5 (Charles F. McCarthy), 6, 7 top (Perry Correll), 7 bottom (Lucian Coman), 8, 10, 11 (DavidXu), 14 (Monkey Business Images), 15 (David Hancock), 16 (Martin Spurny), 18 (Chris Bence), 19 (Bruno Ismael DaSilva Alves), 20 (Gaetano La Bruzzo), 22 top, 22 bottom; US Navy: pp. 9, 23.

Printed in the United States of America at Corporate Graphics
In North Mankato, Minnesota

DAD0502
52011

9 8 7 6 5 4 3 2 1

Contents

Helicopters Everywhere

Rotor

Helicopters are aircraft without wings. A spinning set of blades called a rotor lifts the helicopter into the air.

4

Helicopters can hover (or stay still) in the air. This helicopter is hovering as it **rescues** a man from the ocean.

The Controls

Dials

A helicopter pilot uses levers and pedals to control the helicopter. **Dials** and screens show height, fuel levels, and speed.

Flying a helicopter is a very skilful job.

Pedals

Levers

Pilots use three sets of controls to fly a helicopter. They operate levers with their hands and pedals with their feet.

Big and Small Helicopters

The smallest helicopters can carry just one person.

The big Chinook helicopter has two rotors. It carries very heavy loads. This Chinook is carrying a sling load of **supplies**.

Passenger Helicopters

Helicopters often carry **passengers** over short distances. They can land in very small spaces.

The body of the helicopter is called the fuselage. The pilot and passengers sit in the cabin at the front.

Cabin

Fuselage

Flying Cranes

Helicopters are great for
moving heavy loads. This
flying crane helicopter is
carrying the top of a **pylon**.

A helicopter lifts a load
in a sling attached
underneath. The pilot can
raise and lower the sling.

Air Ambulance

An air ambulance helicopter picks up sick or **injured** people and takes them to the hospital.

Helicopters can reach accidents much faster than ordinary ambulances.

Cops in the Sky

Police forces use helicopters to follow **criminals** trying to escape.

The helicopter pilot tells the police officers on the ground where to go.

Fighting Fires

Firefighters often use helicopters to put out wildfires.

This helicopter is carrying a helibucket. The pilot fills the bucket with water and then dumps it on the fire.

Helibucket

19

Watching the World

A pilot in the air can see many things we cannot see on the ground. Radio and TV crews can record news events from the air.

Filmmakers use helicopters to shoot movie scenes. This helicopter is operated by **remote control**. It has a camera on board.

Fighting Helicopters

Gunships are attack helicopters. They carry machine guns, bombs, and **missiles**.

22

Torpedo

Navy helicopters look for enemy submarines under the water. They attack them with **torpedoes**.

Glossary

criminal	Someone who has done something that is against the law.
dial	A circle with numbers around the edge.
injured	Hurt or harmed.
missile	A weapon that moves through the air and explodes when it reaches its target.
operate	To make a machine work.
passenger	A person who is carried in a plane or helicopter.
pylon	A tall, metal structure that carries overhead electricity cables.
remote control	A device that controls something from a distance.
rescue	To save someone from danger.
supplies	Food and equipment.
torpedo	A tube-shaped bomb that travels underwater and explodes when it hits a target.

Web sites

www.williammaloney.com?Aviation/AmericanHelicopter
Museum/index.htm
Photos of all sorts of helicopters.

http://science.howstuffworks.com/helicopter2.htm
Watch these videos of a helicopter in flight.

www.Exploratorium.edu/science_explorer/roto-copter.html
Make a paper helicopter and test it.

Index